cool drinks
for hot days

cool drinks
for hot days

with recipes by
Louise Pickford

photography by
WILLIAM LINGWOOD

RYLAND
PETERS
& SMALL

LONDON NEW YORK

Designer Iona Hoyle
Commissioning Editor Julia Charles
Picture Research Emily Westlake
Production Toby Marshall
Art Director Leslie Harrington
Publishing Director Alison Starling

Indexer Hilary Bird

First published in the United States in 2009
by Ryland Peters & Small, Inc.
519 Broadway, 5th Floor
New York, NY 10012
www.rylandpeters.com

10 9 8 7 6 5 4 3 2 1

Text © Susannah Blake, Liz Franklin,
Tonia George, Brian Glover, Louise
Pickford, Ben Reed, Sunil Vijayaker,
and Ryland Peters & Small 2009

Design and photographs
© Ryland Peters & Small 2009

ISBN 978 1 84597 847 1

 Library of Congress Cataloging-in-
Publication Data

Pickford, Louise.
  Cool drinks for hot days / with recipes by
Louise Pickford ; photography by William
Lingwood.
     p. cm.
  Includes index.
  ISBN 978-1-84597-847-1
  1. Beverages. I. Title.
  TX815.P533 2009
  641.2--dc22

                            2008048206

Printed in China

Notes
• All spoon measurements are level
unless otherwise specified.
• When using slices of citrus fruit or the
grated peel of lemons and limes in a drink,
try to find organic or unwaxed fruits and
wash well before using. If you can only
find treated fruit, scrub well in warm
soapy water and rinse before using.
• Sterilize cordial bottles before use.
Wash them in hot, soapy water and rinse
in boiling water. Place in a large saucepan
and then cover with hot water. With the lid
on, bring the water to a boil and continue
boiling for 15 minutes. Turn off the heat,
then leave the bottles in the hot water
until just before they are to be filled. Invert
the bottles onto clean paper towels to
dry. Sterilize the lids for 5 minutes, by
boiling, or according to the manufacturer's
instructions. Bottles should be filled with
cordial and sealed while they are still hot.

contents

introduction

The recipes in this book offer the perfect drink for every occasion with a collection of your favorites plus some new ideas. Recipes include classic iced teas, cool summer cocktails, sparkling fruit refreshers, and sophisticated party punches.

It's hardly surprising that many cold drinks came about as a refreshing alternative to their hot counterpart such as tea and coffee. Tea, being the oldest hot drink of all, can be traced back over 5000 years to China. It may have taken centuries before iced tea was invented (or at least documented) but it is now a huge phenomenon particularly in America. One of the first recipes for iced tea appeared in the *Kentucky Housewife* in 1839. However a tea plantation owner named Richard Blechynden is perhaps best known for an inspirational decision to transform his hot tea refreshments into iced tea refreshments during a heat wave at a St. Louis World's Fair in 1904.

Coffee too has it place in a book of cold drinks and is as popular as iced tea. Iced coffee was probably first drunk by the Viennese in the 17th Century due to a surplus of coffee beans. The French added seltzer water to cold coffee around the mid 1800s and named it Mazagran—in reference to a coffee drinking vessel from Mazagran in Algeria. Today iced coffee in all its variations, from non-alcoholic beverages to granitas and cocktails, is drunk in homes, cafés, and bars around the world.

Because the whole aim of cold drinks is to cool us down, they are often alcohol-free. This gives us a wonderful opportunity to create a whole host of delicious mocktails, cordials, fruit syrups, slushies, smoothies, granitas, and pretty much anything else we can combine in a glass. Start the day with a boost of fresh fruit blended to create a deliciously creamy smoothie. Picnics are the ideal place for a homemade cordial. Once made, cordials keep well in a screw top or "stopper" bottle. Just add ice and top up with cold, sparkling water or lemonade for a tangy and refreshing drink.

Once the heat of the day cools to a more manageable balmy evening, fruit cocktails and party punches come into their own and are integral to summer entertaining. Think tall glasses brimming with ice, lemons, oranges, or limes, fresh herbs and even flowers to enhance and tantalize. One of my favorite novels, *The Great Gatsby*, is set in America in the 1920s and will always conjure up images of delicious looking summer drinks sipped by beautiful people in beautiful clothes—romantic scenes indeed. In fact it was during this time of prohibition that the non-alcoholic iced tea was transformed into a deceptively boozy "long" cocktail. The more "creative" drinker found ways to disguise their favorite cocktails to look innocent whilst in truth they were far from it! Long Island iced tea shares just one similarity with its non-alcoholic cousin—the word tea! Packed full of spirits, the small addition of cola as a mixer was purely to help disguise this new drink—anyone drinking this cocktail should be aware it does have a mighty kick!

Finding your favorite drink is easy with each chapter offering the perfect tipple for any occasion. After a hot day in the sun, why not unwind with an iced soft drink from one of those in Iced Teas & Coolers? If you're after something classic then opt for Homemade Fresh Lemonade, but for those yearning for a touch of the exotic, you can't beat a glass of Moroccan Iced Mint Tea or the equally delicious Asian-style Jasmine and Lychee Iced Tea for a thirst-quenching sensation.

Summer never tasted so good as one of the refreshing drinks from Juices, Cordials, & Mocktails proves. Boost energy levels with a fruity homemade cordial such as the antioxidant-packed Blueberry Cordial jazzed up with sparking apple juice or a tangy Pomegranate Squeeze. If it's something elegant and classy for the evening, I love the Cranberry Cooler or what about a spicy Virgin Mary?

Party Drinks & Punches is packed full of fizzy, frothy and fabulous party concoctions. Try a Peach and Strawberry Sangria, tropical Passion Fruit Rum Punch, or the tantalizing Iced Pear Sparkle, all guaranteed to get any party swinging. Of course not all party drinks need to be alcoholic, and there are some lovely fruit punches to be found. My favorite is the Elderflower and Berry Cup where mixed berries are suspended in cubes of ice, adding color and flavor to this delicately perfumed drink.

Summer Cocktails hold a certain romantic nostalgia perhaps because many derive from the 1920s when "the cocktail hour" was an institution. They will certainly add glitz and glamor to your social gatherings and shouldn't be reserved for drinking only when out at a bar. Making your own cocktails at home is great fun and these elegant drinks make balmy summer evenings pure heaven. Try an all-time favorite like the Classic Margarita or a tangy Mint Julep, or experiment with one of the newer inventions like a Chocatini or the dangerously delicious Mandarin Caprioska.

Slushies, Shakes, & Floats provides some fabulous ice-blended drinks, milky concoctions and frozen treats. Cool down in the late afternoon with a Cider Apple Slushie, a Chai Vanilla Milkshake, or a Lemon Ice Cream Soda. There are some wickedly boozy numbers here too, such as the Long Island Milkshake and Mojito Slush.

PRACTICALITIES

You really don't need a great deal to make the perfect summer drink. Of course you'll need ice so that means a freezer is a must. Other than that I'd recommend a good quality blender or liquidizer for the slushies, shakes, and floats and a cocktail shaker for the perfect cocktail. A selection of tall (highball) glasses and classic cocktail glasses, such as the martini or margarita glass, swizzle sticks for stirring drinks, and a selection of straws, as well as large pitchers, punch bowls, and resealable bottles for keeping fruit cordials. The recipes in this book serve 1,2,4, or enough for a party, so always check before shopping so you have enough for whatever you decide to make. I have used 1 oz. as a standard shot for the alcoholic drinks. Some of the drinks can be made ahead (in fact must be made ahead) such as cordials and iced teas, but many are best made just before serving to ensure they are iced and at their tastiest, especially smoothies and blended drinks, as they loose their flavor and nutritional goodness quickly. I hope you have fun with this book—there are so many delicious summer tipples to choose from—but remember with some drinks, a little goes a long way. And, finally, *cheers!*

iced teas & coolers

Make a pitcher of this at the weekend and enjoy throughout the week. The tea you use should have some bitterness and tannins to contrast against the sweetness of both the elderflower and peach juice.

peach & elderflower iced tea

6 black tea bags, such as Keemun or
English Breakfast
6 cups just-boiled water
⅓ cup elderflower cordial
1 cup peach juice
peach slices and raspberries, to serve
ice cubes, to serve

serves 6–8

Put the tea bags in a large heatproof pitcher or bowl and pour in the just-boiled water. Leave to steep for 3–4 minutes, then remove the tea bags and let cool until lukewarm.

Add the elderflower cordial and peach juice and give it a good stir. Leave until cold, then add the peach slices, raspberries, and ice cubes. Pour into tall glasses to serve.

moroccan iced mint tea

1 large bunch of fresh mint leaves
2 cups just-boiled water
sugar, to taste
mint sprigs, to serve
ice cubes, to serve

serves 2

Fill a French press coffee pot with mint, add the just-boiled water and let cool. Carefully push the plunger down, then pour the tea into a pitcher.

Chill, then serve with ice in Moroccan tea glasses, garnished with mint sprigs and offer a separate bowl of sugar.

Pretty-in-pink is a good way of describing this fragrant and mouth-watering concoction, so perfect for a pre-dinner drink on a balmy summer evening. The rose petals are optional but do add a touch of romance.

strawberry, rose, & vanilla iced tea

2 tablespoons strawberry-flavored
tea infusion
1 vanilla bean, split lengthwise
1 quart just-boiled water
2 tablespoons rosewater
1 pint fresh strawberries, hulled
and sliced
clear sparkling lemonade, to top up
rose petals, to garnish (optional)
ice cubes, to serve

serves 6

Place the strawberry tea and vanilla pod in a heatproof pitcher and add the just-boiled water. Stir well and leave to steep until cold. Strain the tea into a clean pitcher and stir in the rosewater.

Put a few ice cubes into 6 tall glasses, add some strawberries and pour over the tea. Top up with lemonade and garnish with a few rose petals, if using, to serve.

mango & berry pash

1 cup frozen mixed berries, thawed
1 tablespoon confectioners' sugar
1 large mango, peeled and pitted
(about 9 oz. flesh)
1 passion fruit, halved
sparkling water, to top up
ice cubes, to serve

serves 2

Put the berries in a bowl and stir in the confectioners' sugar, mashing well with a fork. Set aside for 15 minutes, then pass through a fine strainer. Purée the mango flesh in a blender or liquidizer until smooth and stir in the passion fruit pulp.

Put a few ice cubes into 2 tall glasses, add the berry mixture and mango and passion fruit purée and top up with sparkling water to serve.

iced lime tea

4 tablespoons Chinese Gunpowder
green tea leaves or 3 green tea bags
1 quart just-boiled water
sugar, to taste
1–2 limes, thinly sliced
sparkling water or lemonade, to top up
ice cubes, to serve

serves 4

Put the tea leaves in a warmed teapot
or heatproof pitcher and add the
just-boiled water. Leave to infuse for
5 minutes, then strain the tea into a
clean pitcher. Stir in the sugar, let cool
and then chill.

When ready to serve, add the lime
slices and half-fill the pitcher with ice
cubes. Top up with sparkling water or
lemonade, as preferred, stir to mix and
pour into 4 tall glasses to serve.

I love the rather exotic flavors in this iced tea—if you are lucky enough to find fresh lychees you can use those and simply add a little honey for sweetness, otherwise canned lychees in a light syrup are fine.

jasmine & lychee iced tea

1 tablespoon Jasmine tea leaves
1 quart just-boiled water
2 star anise, bashed lightly
14-oz. can lychees in syrup
lime wedges, to serve
fresh mint leaves, to garnish
clear sparkling lemonade, to top up
ice cubes, to serve

serves 6

Put the tea leaves in a warmed teapot
or heatproof pitcher and pour in the
just-boiled water. Leave to infuse for
5 minutes then strain the tea into a clean
pitcher. Add the star anise and let cool.

Half-fill 6 tall glasses with ice and add
3 lychees and 2 tablespoons of the syrup
to each one. Add a few lime wedges and
mint sprigs to the glasses and top up
with lemonade to serve.

This non-alcoholic refresher is a play on the classic cranberry, grapefruit, and vodka cocktail Sea Breeze (see page 62) but with the cranberry juice frozen into ice cubes. It's fun and funky at the same time.

sea freeze

1 cup cranberry juice
1⅓ cups fresh grapefruit juice
old-fashioned lemonade, to top up
lime slices, to garnish
a 12-hole ice cube tray

serves 2

Pour the cranberry juice into the ice cube tray and freeze for at least 4 hours.

Divide the cubes between 2 tall glasses and add the fresh grapefruit juice. Top up with lemonade and garnish with a slice of lime to serve.

rhubarb berryade

1 lb. rhubarb, trimmed and sliced
2 tablespoons sugar
1 quart just-boiled water
6 strawberries
finely grated peel and freshly squeezed juice of 1 lemon
sparkling water, to top up
ice cubes, to serve

serves 4–8

Put the rhubarb in a saucepan with the sugar and cover with the just-boiled water. Return to a boil, reduce the heat, and stew the rhubarb until it is very soft. Add the strawberries and boil hard for about 1 minute, then strain into a heatproof pitcher and let cool.

Add the grated lemon peel and juice, stir and chill. To serve, pour into tall glasses, add ice and top up with sparkling water.

This is an Australian classic and will always remind me of my first trip down-under. The addition of the bitters is not only a good foil for the sweet drink but adds a pretty pink tinge.

ginger beer, lime, & mint crush

2 limes, each cut into 8 wedges
a handful of fresh mint sprigs
1 teaspoon superfine sugar
2 cups ginger beer
ice cubes, to serve

serves 2

Place the lime, mint, and sugar in a glass pitcher and using a wooden muddler, crush the ingredients together lightly.

Add plenty of ice cubes, top up with ginger beer, and pour into 2 tall glasses to serve.

lemon, lime, & bitters

a handful of fresh mint sprigs
2 limes, each cut into 8 wedges
1 quart clear sparkling lemonade
50 ml lime cordial
a dash of angostura bitters
ice cubes, to serve

serves 6

Half-fill 6 tall glasses with ice and add a sprig of mint and 2–3 lime wedges to each one.

Pour in the lemonade and lime cordial and add a few drops of bitters to serve.

I think of iced teas as a typical Louisiana-style refreshment. Tall, elegant glasses filled with ice, and of course iced tea is a drink that's well suited to the grand colonial homes prevalent in this part of the US. Fresh peaches or nectarines can be used instead of apricots.

iced Louisiana apricot tea

4 orange pekoe tea bags
2 sprigs of fresh rosemary
1 quart just-boiled water
1⅓ cups apricot nectar
6 fresh apricots, halved, pitted, and sliced
sparkling water, to top up
rosemary sprigs, to garnish
ice cubes, to serve

serves 6

Put the tea bags and rosemary in a heatproof pitcher and pour in the just-boiled water. Leave to steep for 10 minutes, then remove and discard the tea bags. Let cool then chill for 1 hour and then remove and discard the rosemary.

Stir in the apricot nectar, apricots, and ice cubes and pour into tall glasses. Top up each drink with sparkling water and garnish with a sprig of rosemary to serve.

cranberry, lemon, & ginger iced tea

4 lemon and ginger-flavored tea bags
1 quart just-boiled water
2 teaspoons brown sugar
1½ cups cranberry juice
1 lemon, sliced
lemon balm leaves, to garnish
ice cubes, to serve

serves 6

Put the tea bags in a heatproof pitcher and pour in the just-boiled water. Leave to steep for about 10 minutes, then remove and discard the tea bags. Stir in the sugar and let cool. Chill for 1 hour.

Stir in the cranberry juice and add the lemon slices and lemon balm. Divide between tall, ice-filled glasses to serve.

Fresh lemonade is simple to make and you can keep the lemony syrup in the fridge and dilute it with either chilled sparkling water or soda water as required. A Spanish cook I once knew used to add saffron to her lemonade to make a golden-hued drink with an intriguing taste. Just add a pinch of saffron threads to the warm syrup when you take it off the heat.

homemade fresh lemonade

thinly pared peel and freshly squeezed
juice of 6 large lemons
¾ cup sugar
2½ cups water
fresh lemon slices, to serve
sprigs of fresh mint, to serve
sparkling water, to top up
ice cubes, to serve

serves 6–8

Put the grated lemon peel, sugar, and water in a saucepan and bring slowly to a simmer, stirring to dissolve the sugar. As soon as the sugar is dissolved and the syrup begins to bubble, take it off the heat. Half-cover and leave until cold.

Squeeze the lemons and add the juice to the cold syrup. Strain into a bowl, cover and chill.

Transfer the lemonade to a glass pitcher filled with ice cubes and add the lemon slices and mint. Dilute with sparkling water on a ratio of about 1 part syrup to 1 part water.

apple lemonade

2–3 cooking apples, unpeeled and
chopped into small pieces
sugar, to taste
freshly squeezed juice of 1 lemon
sparkling water, to top up
ice cubes, to serve

serves 4

Put the apples in a saucepan, cover with cold water, bring to a boil, and simmer until soft. Strain the juice into a bowl, pressing the pulp through a strainer with a spoon. Discard any pulp that stays in the strainer. Sweeten the apple juice to taste and let cool.

To serve, fill a pitcher with ice cubes, pour in the apple juice, add the lemon juice, and top up with sparkling water. Pour into 4 tall glasses to serve.

juices, cordials, & mocktails

It's so simple. I defy anyone not to admit that a Cranberry Cooler, when served ice cold and in the right proportions, is the only thing that almost beats a lemonade made just right! The St. Clement's takes its name from the English nursery rhyme "Oranges and Lemons said the bells of St. Clement's."

cranberry cooler

1 cup soda water
1 cup cranberry juice
freshly squeezed lime juice, to taste
crushed ice, to serve

serves 2

Fill 2 tall glasses with crushed ice. Pour in equal parts of soda water and then cranberry juice. Add a squeeze or two of lime juice to taste and serve.

st. clement's

1 cup bitter lemon
1 cup fresh orange juice
lemon slices, to garnish
ice cubes, to serve

serves 2

Fill 2 tall glasses with ice cubes. Pour in equal parts of bitter lemon and orange juice. Stir gently, garnish each drink with a lemon slice, and serve.

*Pomegranate syrup is a Middle Eastern
condiment used in cooking. It has a rather
wonderful sweet-sour flavor that is hard to
define yet totally delicious. There isn't really
a true substitute so I recommend tracking
down a bottle from a specialist food supplier.*

pomegranate syrup & lemonade

1 teaspoon pomegranate syrup
lemon slices, to garnish
a sprig of fresh mint
clear sparkling lemonade, to top up
ice cubes, to serve

serves 1

Put a few ice cubes in a tall glass. Add
the pomegranate syrup, lemon slices,
and mint and top up with lemonade.
Stir well before serving.

pomegranate squeeze

3 fresh pomegranates
1 tablespoon grenadine (optional)
freshly squeezed juice of 1 orange
ice cubes, to serve

serves 1

Use a very sharp knife to cut the
pomegranates in half around the middle.
Using a lemon squeezer, squeeze the
juice from them. Put a few ice cubes
in a tall glass. Add the grenadine, if
using, then pour in both the orange
and pomegranate juices. Stir gently
before serving.

fruity ice sticks

Make pretty, flavored decorations for your drinks or a large punch-bowl by adding slices of fruit or berries to novelty ice trays, topping up with water and freezing until firm.

suggested ice-shape ingredients
berries:
blackberries, whole
raspberries, whole
small strawberries, whole
blueberries, whole
red, black, and white currants

fruit:
star-fruit, sliced
lemons, sliced
oranges, sliced
kiwi fruit, sliced
green, red, or black seedless grapes, whole or sliced

Making your own cordials or fruit syrups is so satisfying as with very little effort you have a delicious fruit drink mixer that will last you for ages. You could use other berries, such as blackberries or raspberries, and top up with still or sparkling water or clear lemonade.

blueberry cordial with apple fizz

1¾ cups frozen blueberries
1 cup sugar
sparkling apple juice, to top up
ice cubes, to serve

makes 2 cups cordial

❄

Place the blueberries and sugar in a large saucepan and heat gently until the blueberries soften and the sugar dissolves. Bring to a boil and simmer over a medium heat for 15 minutes, until syrupy.

Strain through a fine strainer and pour into a sterilized bottle (see note on page 4). Seal and leave to cool.

To serve, pour 2–3 tablespoons of cordial into tall glasses, add a few ice cubes and top up with sparkling apple juice. The cordial will keep in the fridge for 4 weeks.

I love the combination of orange and passion fruit so this is one of my favorite cordials. If you like the pretty black seeds of the passion fruit, leave the cordial unstrained.

passion fruit & orange cordial

finely pared peel of 1 orange
2 cups sugar
1 cup fresh orange juice
½ cup passion fruit pulp
½ teaspoon citric acid
still or sparkling water, to top up
ice cubes, to serve

makes 2 cups cordial

Put the orange peel and sugar in a large saucepan with the orange juice, passion fruit pulp, and citric acid. Set over a low heat and stir until the sugar is dissolved. Bring to a boil and remove from the heat. Leave to cool completely, strain and then transfer to a sterilized bottle (see note on page 4).

To serve, pour 2–3 tablespoons of cordial into tall glasses, add a few ice cubes and top up with still or sparkling water, as preferred. The cordial will keep in the fridge for 4 weeks.

This vibrant and deliciously tangy juice is reminiscent of the classic cocktail Tequila Sunrise but without the alcohol.

orange sunset

6 oranges
2 pomegranates
ice cubes, to serve
an electric juicer

serves 2

Peel the oranges, chop the flesh, and press through an electric juicer into a pitcher. Halve the pomegranates and, using a lemon squeezer, squeeze out the juice into a separate pitcher.

Pour the orange juice into 2 ice-filled glasses or tumblers, then pour in the pomegranate juice in a thin stream. Serve immediately.

This is a deliciously fruity concoction. Apricots are very dense so you may like to pulp them in a blender or liquidizer rather than putting them through an electric juicer. If you do decide to juice them, remove the skins first (see note below).

blueberry & orange juice

4 oranges
1 pint fresh blueberries
ice cubes, to serve
an electric juicer

serves 1—2

Squeeze the oranges, then put the juice in a blender or liquidizer with the blueberries and whizz until smooth.

Alternatively, peel the oranges, then chop the flesh and feed half of it through an electric juicer, followed by the blueberries, then the remaining orange flesh.

Pour into ice-filled glasses or tumblers to serve.

apricot, strawberry, & orange juice

2 oranges
8 ripe fresh apricots, halved, pitted, and coarsely chopped
8 strawberries, hulled and halved
ice cubes, to serve
an electric juicer (optional)

serves 1—2

Squeeze the oranges and put the juice in a blender or liquidizer with the apricots and strawberries. Whizz until smooth, adding a little water if needed. If the mixture is still too thick, add a few ice cubes and whizz again. Pour into ice-filled glasses or tumblers to serve.

Note To remove the skins from the apricots, bring a saucepan of water to a boil, add the whole apricots and blanch them for about 1 minute. Drain and when cool enough to handle, pull off the skins using the back of a knife.

This is a truly refreshing drink for a hot summer's day, and with the addition of the sparkling water it makes a delightful non-alcoholic cocktail.

raspberry & apple fizz

1¾ cups frozen raspberries
1 cup apple juice
sparkling water, to top up
ice cubes
serves 4

Put the raspberries, apple juice, and about 12 ice cubes in a blender or liquidizer and whizz until smooth. Pour into 4 tall glasses and top up with sparkling water to serve.

These delightfully cooling iced treats are known as "golas" in India, where they are enjoyed on the hottest of days.

crushed ice sticks with fruit cordial

1–2 cups finely crushed ice
any fruit-based syrup or cordial such as blueberry, strawberry, elderflower, rose, lemon, orange, or black currant
6 short wooden or bamboo skewers
serves 6

Take about 2 oz. crushed ice in the palm of your hand and mold it around the end of a wooden or bamboo skewer, pressing tightly so the ice forms into a rough popsicle shape.

Fill small glasses (shot glasses are ideal) with the syrup of your choice. To eat, dip the ice stick into the syrup and then suck the syrup through the ice. Keep dipping until the ice is gone.

raspberry, apple, & lychee juice

14-oz. can lychees in syrup
1 cup frozen raspberries
1 cup apple juice
ice cubes, to serve

serves 2

Drain the lychees and reserve the syrup. Put them in a blender or liquidizer and add the raspberries and apple juice. Whizz until smooth. If the juice is too thick, add a little of the lychee syrup to thin.

Divide the juice between 2 ice-filled glasses or tumblers to serve.

This is an instant berry cordial that fizzes and refreshes. Use any combination of berries you like and if you can't find fresh berries just substitute thawed frozen berries instead.

berry cordial

2 pints fresh mixed berries, such as raspberries, strawberries, blueberries and blackcurrants
½ cup sugar syrup
freshly squeezed juice of ½ lime
sparkling water, to top up
a few whole berries, to garnish
ice cubes, to serve

serves 4

Place the berries, sugar syrup, and lime juice in a blender or liquidizer and whizz until smooth. Pass the mixture through a fine strainer and divide the cordial between 4 tall glasses.

Add ice cubes, top up with sparkling water and garnish with a few berries to serve.

Juicy melon and cool cucumber are blended to make a super-cooling and satisfying summer drink, and stem ginger adds a nice spicy kick. Ginger also works well here with the pear juice—the two flavors just seem to have a natural affinity.

melon, cucumber, & ginger frappé

½ galia melon
½ cucumber
1 tablespoon chopped stem ginger, plus 1 tablespoon syrup from the jar
freshly squeezed juice of ½ lime
ice cubes

serves 2

Seed the melon and scoop the flesh into a blender or liquidizer.

Peel and chop the cucumber and add to the blender along with the stem ginger, reserved syrup, lime juice, and about 6 ice cubes. Whizz until smooth.

Divide the mixture between 2 glasses or tumblers to serve.

gingered pear juice

1 small papaya, about 12 oz.
14 oz. cantaloupe melon
1 cup pear juice
freshly squeezed juice of 1 lime
1 teaspoon grated fresh ginger
ice cubes, to serve

serves 2

Peel the papaya and cut it in half, scoop out and discard the seeds and then chop the flesh.

Seed the melon and scoop out the flesh. Put the papaya and melon in a blender or liquidizer along with the pear and lime juices and grated ginger. Whizz until smooth.

Divide the juice between 2 ice-filled glasses or tumblers to serve.

Here in Australia watermelons are super tasty and sweet. This is delicious enjoyed after a day at the beach or watching the sun set behind the ocean waves.

watermelon kick

7 oz. watermelon, seeded and diced watermelon
1 oz. lime cordial
½ cup pink grapefruit juice
tonic water, to top up
ice cubes, to serve

serves 2

Put the watermelon and lime cordial in a blender or liquidizer and whizz until smooth.

Put a few ice cubes into 2 tall glasses, add half the watermelon mixture and half the grapefruit juice. Top up with tonic water and serve.

A perfectly ripe mango is aromatic, with a heavenly flavor and silky texture. Combined here with raspberries and cranberry juice, it becomes an even more delicious treat.

mango, raspberry, & cranberry cruise

1 large mango, about 1 lb., peeled
1 cup frozen raspberries
1 cup cranberry juice
1 teaspoon runny honey, to taste
ice cubes, to serve

serves 2

Cut down each side of the mango pit and dice the flesh. Put in a blender or liquidizer and add the raspberries and cranberry juice. Whizz until smooth. Taste and add a teaspoon of honey to sweeten, if necessary.

Divide between 2 ice-filled glasses or tumblers to serve.

These four melon varieties are all very aromatic. My juicer produces a froth, but if yours is less muscular, you could layer the juices to form orange and green stripes. This is a great drink for a summer lunch party.

sweet melon frothy

1 orange-fleshed melon, such as cantaloupe or charentais
1 green-fleshed melon, such as galia or honeydew
ginger syrup, to taste
an electric juicer (optional)

serves 1-2

Halve and seed the melons then slice the flesh from the skin. Keep the 2 types of melon separate.

If you have an electric juicer, feed the melon pieces through it. Alternatively, dice the flesh and put it in a blender or liquidizer. Whizz until smooth.

Layer the orange and green juices in glasses or tumblers, or serve them separately if preferred. Serve the ginger syrup separately as a sweetener.

This interesting combination of thin yet fragrant watermelon juice and the thick, almost chalky pear juice is perfect. Try it!

watermelon & pear frothy

3 pears
2-lb. wedge watermelon
ice cubes, to serve
an electric juicer

serves 2-3

Cut the pears into pieces small enough to fit through the funnel of an electric juicer and press through into a pitcher.

Cut the watermelon flesh into chunks. Put it in a blender or liquidizer with the pear juice and whizz until smooth. Pour the juice into 2 ice-filled glasses to serve.

There's nothing in the manual that says a no-alcohol cocktail should be low maintenance. The Virgin Mary is a good way of saying thank you to anyone who has taken on the noble role of designated driver for the night. Since this variation is without vodka, you can go a bit crazy on the spices to compensate!

virgin mary

1¼ cups tomato juice
2 grinds of black pepper
2 dashes Tabasco sauce
2 dashes Worcestershire sauce
2 dashes freshly squeezed lemon juice
¼–½ teaspoon horseradish sauce,
to taste
ice cubes, to serve
a celery rib, to garnish

serves 1

Fill a cocktail shaker with ice. Add the tomato juice and all of the seasonings. Shake to combine, then strain into a tall, ice-filled glass and garnish with a celery rib to serve.

The Shirley Temple is an alcohol-free mocktail that's named after the famous Hollywood child actress. I imagine this pretty drink got its name because of its sweetness and candy color, both of which make it a popular choice with kids.

shirley temple

1 oz. grenadine
ginger ale or clear sparkling lemonade,
to top up
lemon slices, to garnish
ice cubes, to serve

serves 6

Pour the grenadine into 6 tall, ice-filled glasses and top up with either ginger ale or lemonade, as preferred. Garnish each with a slice of lemon to serve.

party drinks
& punches

This traditional English summertime drink is perfect for entertaining.

pimms

1 part Pimms
3 parts clear sparkling lemonade
cucumber slices
lemon slices
orange slices
strawberries, hulled (optional)
sprigs of fresh mint
ice cubes, to serve

serves 1

Take a tall glass (or large pitcher) and half-fill with ice. Add the Pimm's and lemonade and gently stir. Add the cucumber, lemon and orange slices, and strawberries (if using) and garnish with the mint.

iced pear sparkle

1 teaspoon runny honey
1 oz. pear liqueur
1 oz. Cointreau, or other orange-flavored liqueur
¼ pear (nashi if available), peeled and thinly sliced
champagne or sparkling white wine
ice cubes, to serve

serves 1

Put the honey and some ice in a cocktail shaker and gently crush with a wooden muddler. Add the pear liqueur and Cointreau, replace the lid and shake briskly but briefly.

Pour into a chilled glass, add some pear slices, and top up with champagne. Serve immediately.

This colorful, fruity punch will delight children and adults alike. Of course for those who just love a little extra pizzazz, you could always add a shot or two of vodka!

cranberry & fruit punch

2 pints mixed fresh berries, such as strawberries, raspberries, and blueberries
1 orange, sliced
2 quarts cranberry juice
1 small cucumber, peeled, seeded, and sliced
sparkling water or clear sparkling lemonade, to top up
ice cubes, to serve

serves 12

Put the berries, orange slices, and cranberry juice in a large pitcher and chill for 1 hour.

When ready to serve, add the cucumber and some ice and top up with sparkling water. Pour into tall glasses or tumblers to serve.

passion fruit rum punch

This has a distinctly Caribbean flavor. You could use golden rum but I prefer the slightly more delicate taste of white rum.

1 cup white rum
½ cup passion fruit pulp (from about 6 large ripe passion fruit)
½ cup fresh orange juice
2 cups clear sparkling lemonade
ice cubes, to serve

serves 6

Put the rum, passion fruit pulp, and orange juice in a large pitcher and chill for 1 hour.

Half-fill 6 tall glasses with ice, add the rum and fruit juice mixture, and top up with lemonade. Serve immediately.

The berry ice cubes give this drink a pretty party feel. I make it up in a large pitcher and let it sit for 10 minutes before serving—the ice cubes begin to melt, coloring the drink a delicate pink with the berry juices.

elderflower & berry cup

1 pint mixed berries, such as
raspberries, strawberries, and
blueberries
½ cup elderflower cordial
sparkling water, to top up
elderflowers, to garnish (optional)
an ice cube tray

serves 4

Divide the berries between the ice cube tray holes and top up with still water. Freeze for 2 hours or until frozen.

Unmold the ice cubes into a large pitcher or 4 tall glasses and pour in the elderflower cordial. Top up with sparkling water, garnish with a few elderflowers, if using, and serve.

alabama slammer

Slammers are a style of drink that's always great entertainment at a party. A small word of warning though, they are pretty potent and should be consumed in moderation.

1 oz. Southern Comfort or bourbon
chilled champagne

serves 1

Pour the Southern Comfort and champagne into a sturdy shot glass.

Place your hand over the top and then firmly but carefully slam the bottom of the glass on the counter top. The drink will fizz up and should be drunk immediately and all at once!

Martinis never tasted or looked so good! Each fruit quantity will make four drinks, so choose whichever flavor you prefer—or why not try one of each?

fruit martinis

9 oz. kiwi fruit (about 4 kiwi fruit)
9 oz. strawberries
9 oz. watermelon (peeled weight)
3 tablespoons superfine sugar
1 cup iced vodka
kiwi slices, strawberries and small watermelon wedges, to garnish
ice cubes, lightly crushed, to serve

serves 4–12, as desired

✳

Peel and chop the kiwi fruit, hull and halve the strawberries, and roughly chop the watermelon.

Purée each fruit separately in a blender or liquidizer with 1 tablespoon sugar, until really smooth. Set aside.

Put each fruit purée separately into a cocktail shaker and add ⅓ cup iced vodka and a little crushed ice. Replace the lid and shake vigorously for about 30 seconds, remove the lid and pour into 4 martini glasses. Decorate each glass with a slice of the fruit used and serve immediately.

hollywood hustle

This fizzy little tipple is guaranteed to kick-start any big night out!

1 oz. citron vodka
⅓ cup Red Bull or other sparkling energy drink
⅓ cup champagne
crushed ice, to serve

serves 1

✳

Fill a chilled tumbler with crushed ice and pour over the citron vodka. Top up with the Red Bull and champagne and serve immediately.

A fragrant and more delicate version of the Spanish Classic Sangria (see page 55). You can add almost any fruit you like and vary the liqueur. Try peach schnapps or crème de framboise (raspberry-flavored liqueur).

hamptons hangover

This fragrant summer cocktail gets it's delicate flavor and pretty color from black currant liqueur and rose syrup.

1 oz. Crème de Cassis (black currant-flavored liqueur)
2 oz. rose syrup, such as Monin
1 oz. freshly squeezed lemon juice
clear sparkling lemonade, to top up
ice cubes, to serve

serves 1

Half-fill a tumbler with ice. Add the cassis, rose syrup, and lemon juice. Top up with lemonade and stir gently before serving.

peach & strawberry sangria

2 fresh peaches, pitted and thinly sliced
1 pint strawberries, hulled and sliced
1 orange, sliced
⅔ cup Crème de Fraise (strawberry-flavored liqueur)
2 x 750-ml bottles (6 cups) white wine
1 small cucumber, peeled, seeded, and thinly sliced
clear sparkling lemonade, to top up
borage flowers, to garnish (optional)
ice cubes, to serve

serves 12

Put the peaches, strawberries, and orange slices in a large pitcher with the strawberry liqueur. Pour in the wine and chill for 30 minutes. When ready to serve, add the cucumber and some ice and top up with lemonade. Pour into glasses and garnish each serving with borage flowers, if using.

I love this delicious summer punch—it is the perfect drink for a balmy evening, especially if you are lucky enough to find yourself sitting by the sea. It will always remind me of great holidays spent in Majorca, where people relax in the beach bars with large jugs of it.

classic sangria

2 oranges, sliced
2 lemons, sliced
1–2 tablespoons sugar, to taste
2 x 750-ml bottles (6 cups) red wine
⅔ cup Grand Marnier or other
orange-flavored liqueur
1 eating apple, sliced into thin wedges
clear sparkling lemonade, to top up
ice cubes, to serve

serves 12

Place half the orange and lemon slices in a large pitcher and sprinkle over the sugar. Leave to macerate for 15 minutes then add the wine and Grand Marnier and chill for 1 hour.

When ready to serve, add the apple wedges and remaining orange and lemon slices. Add a few scoops of ice and top up with lemonade to taste. Stir and pour into tall glasses to serve, spooning a little fruit into each, if liked.

gingerella punch

1½ lbs. mixed melon flesh, such as
watermelon, honeydew, and galia, diced
750-ml bottle (6 cups) ginger wine, such
as Stone's or Crabbie's
dry ginger ale, to top up
a handful of small fresh basil leaves,
to garnish
ice cubes, to serve

serves 12

Put the melon and ginger wine in a large pitcher and chill for 1 hour.

When ready to serve, transfer to a punch bowl and add a few scoops of ice, pour in the ginger ale to taste and add the basil leaves. Ladle into tumblers or wine goblets to serve, spooning a little melon into each, if liked.

summer cocktails

The secret to making a great Mai Tai is to use a thick, dark rum. It's a fresh and fruity drink, perfect for sipping as you relax by the pool.

mai tai

2 oz. dark rum, ideally aged Demerara
½ oz. triple sec
½ oz. apricot brandy
½ oz. freshly squeezed lemon or lime juice
a dash of angostura bitters
2 dashes of Orgeat syrup (bitter almond-flavored syrup)
½ oz. fresh pineapple juice
a fresh mint sprig, to garnish
ice cubes, to serve

serves 1

Put all the ingredients, except the mint garnish, in a cocktail shaker filled with ice, shake vigorously but briefly, then strain into an ice-filled glass. Garnish with a mint sprig and serve immediately.

mint julep

This reviving, tongue-tingling cocktail originated in the American deep south where they know a thing or two about keeping cool in hot weather.

5 sprigs of fresh mint
2 sugar cubes
2 oz. bourbon or white or dark rum, if preferred
crushed ice, to serve

serves 1

Crush the mint and sugar cubes in the bottom of a heavy-based glass with a wooden muddler.

Fill the glass with crushed ice and add the bourbon. Stir the mixture vigorously and serve immediately.

Here are two delicious cocktails for chocolate lovers. Served ice-cold, they are a great way to enjoy the taste of chocolate on warm days without it melting all over your hands!

chocmint martini

2 oz. vodka
1 oz. crème de cacao
½ oz. crème de menthe
ice cubes

serves 1

Fill a cocktail shaker with ice. Add the vodka, crème de cacao, and crème de menthe. Replace the lid and shake briskly. Strain into a frosted martini glass and serve immediately.

chocatini

1 oz. dark chocolate
2 oz. vodka
1½ oz. crème de cacao
ice cubes

serves 1

Melt the chocolate by placing it in a heatproof bowl set over a saucepan of just-simmering water (do not let the bowl touch the water). Stir until melted.

Transfer the melted chocolate to a plate. Take a martini glass and carefully dip the rim into the melted chocolate to give a thin line of chocolate. Invert and put in the fridge to set for 20 minutes.

Fill a cocktail shaker with ice. Add the vodka and crème de cacao and shake vigorously but briefly. Strain into the chilled, chocolate-rimmed glass and serve immediately.

Both these long summer drinks were made for sipping on a shady verandah or porch at the end of a long, hot day.

long island iced tea

1 oz. vodka
1 oz. gin
1 oz. white rum
1 oz. tequila
1 oz. triple sec
½ oz. freshly squeezed lemon juice
½ oz. sugar syrup
cola, to top up
lemon slices, to serve
ice cubes, to serve

serves 1

Fill a cocktail shaker with ice and add all of the ingredients except the cola. Shake briskly, then pour into a tall glass. Top up with a splash of cola, add a few lemon slices and some more ice, if liked. Serve immediately.

rum runner

1 oz. white rum
1 oz. dark rum
freshly squeezed juice of 1 lime
a dash of sugar syrup
⅔ cup fresh pineapple juice
crushed ice, to serve

serves 1

Fill a cocktail shaker with ice. Add all the ingredients and shake vigorously but briefly. Strain into a tall glass filled with crushed ice and serve immediately.

Cranberry juice lends a light, fruity, refreshing quality to both these cocktails—slightly bitter in the Sea Breeze but softened in the Cosmopolitan Iced Tea by the triple sec.

cosmopolitan iced tea

1 oz. vodka, vanilla-flavored
if available
½ oz. triple sec
⅓ cup cranberry juice
freshly squeezed juice of ½ lime
ice cubes, to serve

serves 1

Fill a cocktail shaker with ice. Add the vodka, triple sec, and cranberry and lime juices. Replace the lid and shake briskly. Strain into a tall glass, half-filled with ice. Serve immediately.

sea breeze

1 oz. vodka
⅔ cup cranberry juice
¼ cup fresh grapefruit juice
a lime wedge, to garnish
ice cubes, to serve

serves 1

Half-fill a tall glass with ice. Pour in the vodka and add the cranberry and grapefruit juices. Stir and garnish with a lime wedge. Serve immediately.

Both these drinks are great for those who enjoy a sharp citrus taste softened a little with sugar. The Tennessee Teaser is a variation on the more familiar Cuba Libre and the Daiquiri is a classic cocktail that was made famous at the El Floridita restaurant in Havana.

tennessee teaser

2 oz. Jack Daniels, or other bourbon
1 oz. freshly squeezed lemon juice
½ oz. sugar syrup
cola, to top up
a dash of angostura bitters
ice cubes, to serve

serves 1

Half-fill a glass with ice. Add the Jack Daniels, lemon juice, and sugar syrup and top up with cola. Add a dash of bitters and serve immediately.

original daiquiri

2 oz. golden rum
1 oz. freshly squeezed lime juice
2 teaspoons sugar syrup
ice cubes

serves 1

Fill a cocktail shaker with ice. Add all the ingredients, replace the lid and shake briskly. Strain into a chilled glass and serve immediately.

Rum has a great affinity with fresh juices and the ability to hold its own when combined with quite a selection of other flavors. This delicious long drink is packed with fruity cranberry and pineapple juice and given a bit of extra zing with spicy fresh ginger.

jamaican breeze

2 oz. white rum
2 slices of fresh ginger
⅓ cup cranberry juice
⅓ cup fresh pineapple juice
ice cubes, to serve

serves 1

❅

Put the rum and ginger together in the bottom of a cocktail shaker and pound with a wooden muddler. Add ice to the shaker, pour in the cranberry and pineapple juices. Shake briskly, then strain into a tall glass filled with ice. Serve immediately.

Although mandarin season is traditionally winter, like lemons and limes, mandarins are now available most of the year. So this is actually the perfect summertime cocktail—it seems to work well with smoky grilled food. Use tangerines or oranges when mandarins are unavailable.

mandarin caprioska

1 mandarin, cut into wedges
fresh mint leaves, torn
1 oz. triple sec
1 oz. vodka
tonic water, to top up
ice cubes, to serve

serves 1

❅

Put the mandarin wedges, mint leaves, and ice into a chilled glass, squeezing the mandarin wedges as you go to release their juices. Pour over the triple sec and vodka, then top up with tonic water to serve.

These summery alternatives to the classic Moscow Mule, while being completely different in taste, still use the basic Mule ingredients, namely ginger beer and vodka. The Strawberry Mule is perfect for an afternoon in the sun, while the Brazilian Mule is great after dinner.

strawberry mule

3 strawberries plus 1 extra to garnish
2 thin slices of fresh ginger
2 oz. vodka
1 oz. Crème de Fraise (strawberry-flavored liqueur)
a dash of sugar syrup
ginger beer, to top up
ice cubes, to serve

serves 1

Put the ginger and strawberries together in a cocktail shaker and pound with a wooden muddler. Add the vodka, strawberry liqueur, and sugar syrup and replace the lid. Shake briskly, then strain into a tall glass filled with ice. Top up with ginger beer, stir gently and garnish with a strawberry to serve.

brazilian mule

1 oz. vodka
½ oz. peppermint schnapps
½ oz. ginger wine, such as Stone's or Crabbie's
1 oz. (a shot) strong, freshly-made espresso coffee
a dash of sugar syrup
ginger beer, to top up
coffee beans, to garnish (optional)
ice cubes, to serve

serves 1

Fill a cocktail shaker with ice. Add the vodka, peppermint schnapps, and ginger wine. Pour in the espresso coffee and add sugar syrup to taste. Replace the lid and shake briskly. Strain into a tall glass filled with ice and top up with ginger beer. Garnish with coffee beans, if using, and serve.

Although this recipe for Planter's Punch makes one serving, it is also a great drink for parties because it can be made in advance. Make it in a large bowl and add slices of fresh fruit, such as oranges, apples, and pears. T-Punch is an equally tangy and refreshing drink, just perfect for sipping on a hot summer's day.

planter's punch

2 oz. dark rum
freshly squeezed juice of ½ lemon
2 oz. fresh orange juice
a dash of sugar syrup
club soda, to top up
an orange slice, to garnish
ice cubes, to serve

serves 1

Fill a cocktail shaker with ice and add the rum, lemon and orange juices, and sugar syrup. Replace the lid and shake briskly. Strain into an ice-filled tall glass. Top up with club soda and garnish with a slice of orange to serve.

t-punch

1 brown sugar cube
1 lime
2 oz. white rum
club soda, to top up
ice cubes, to serve

serves 1

Put the sugar cube in the bottom of a heavy-based tumbler. Cut the lime into eighths, squeeze and drop into the glass. Crush gently with a wooden muddler to break up the sugar. Add the rum and ice, then top up with club soda. Stir and serve immediately.

The Mojito, with its alluring mix of mint and rum, whisks its drinker away to warmer climes. Wildly popular in Miami for years, this Cuban concoction can now be found gracing the menus of cocktail bars around the world, along with the equally trendy Caipirinha.

caipirinha

1 lime
2 brown sugar cubes
2 oz. cachaça
crushed ice, to serve

serves 1

Cut the lime into eighths, squeeze and place in a heavy-based tumbler with the sugar cubes. Crush well with a wooden muddler. Fill the glass with crushed ice and add the cachaça. Stir well and serve with two short straws.

mojito

5 sprigs of fresh mint
2 oz. golden rum
a squeeze of fresh lime juice
2 dashes of sugar syrup
club soda, to top up
crushed ice, to serve

serves 1

Put the mint in a tall glass, add the rum, lime juice, and sugar syrup. Crush with a long-handled spoon until the aroma of the mint is released. Add some crushed ice and stir vigorously until the mixture and the mint are spread evenly. Top up with club soda and stir again. Serve with two straws.

The key to a perfect Margarita is good-quality tequila, so do invest in a recognised brand. I've included a fun twist on the classic here—the Mangorita. It's delicious and easy to make but very tricky to get just right as the mango flavor can overshadow the taste of tequila. Take care not to add too much mango purée.

mangorita

2 oz. gold tequila
1 oz. triple sec
1 oz. freshly squeezed lime juice
½–1 oz. fresh mango purée
ice cubes

serves 1

Fill a cocktail shaker with ice. Add the tequila, triple sec, lime juice, and mango purée. Replace the lid and shake briskly. Strain into a frosted margarita glass and serve immediately.

classic margarita

2 oz. gold tequila
1 oz. triple sec
½–1 oz. freshly squeezed lime juice
sea salt, for the rim of the glass
a lime slice, to garnish
ice cubes

serves 1

Fill a cocktail shaker with ice. Add the tequila, triple sec, and lime juice. Replace the lid and shake briskly. Strain into a salt-rimmed, frosted margarita glass and garnish with a lime slice. Serve immediately.

Variation: For a Frozen Margarita, put all the ingredients (except the garnish) in a blender or liquidizer, add one scoop of crushed ice and whizz for 20 seconds. Pour into a margarita glass and garnish with a lime slice. Serve immediately.

There seems to be something about raspberries in cocktails that everyone enjoys, so a long Raspberry Rickey is guaranteed to be a popular summer cooler. Try the Vodka Collins for a sharper, more zingy, thirst-quencher but be warned, it's easy to forget there is alcohol in both these deceptively soft-tasting drinks.

raspberry rickey

4 fresh raspberries, plus 1 to garnish
2 oz. vodka
1 oz. freshly squeezed lime juice
a dash of Chambord, or other
raspberry-flavored liqueur
club soda, to top up
ice cubes, to serve

serves 1

Put the raspberries in the bottom of
a tall glass and squash with a wooden
muddler or long-handled spoon. Fill
the glass with ice and add the vodka,
lime juice, and Chambord. Top up
with club soda and stir. Garnish with
a raspberry to serve.

vodka collins

2 oz. vodka
1 oz. freshly squeezed lemon juice
1 tablespoon sugar syrup
club soda, to top up
lemon slices, to garnish
ice cubes, to serve

serves 1

Fill a tall glass with ice and add the
vodka, lemon juice, and sugar syrup.
Top up with club soda, stir gently
and garnish with lemon slices to serve.

slushies, shakes, & floats

This light, frothy and refreshing blend is the perfect antidote to a hot summer's afternoon. For that extra kick, add a spoonful of Kahlúa.

frothy iced coffee

1 cup crushed ice
½ cup full-fat milk
2 oz. freshly-brewed espresso coffee
1 tablespoon superfine sugar
a scoop of vanilla ice cream

serves 1

Put the ice in a blender or liquidizer.
Add the milk, espresso, and sugar and
whizz for about 30 seconds, until frothy
and slushy. Pour into a tall glass and top
with the ice cream. Serve immediately.

ice cream ice cubes *for* sodas

Drop these ice cream ice cubes into tall glasses of clear lemonade or other soda—to create old-fashioned ice cream sodas.

9 oz. mascarpone cheese
1⅓ cup full-fat milk
½ cup superfine sugar
ice cube trays

makes 18-24
depending on size of ice cube
trays used

Put the mascarpone, milk, and sugar
in a bowl and use a hand-held electric
whisk to blend until thick and smooth.
Use a spoon to transfer the mixture to
ice cube trays and freeze until solid.

I couldn't resist a reference to Australia's most famous beach in this book of summer drinks. After all there are few better ways of watching the world go by than sipping fruit shakes or cocktails as the heat of the day fades and the sun worshippers head home for the night.

bondi rip

1 large mango, peeled, pitted, and diced
1 banana, peeled and sliced
1 cup pineapple juice
2 oz. raspberry syrup
ice cubes

serves 2

❄

Put the mango, banana, and pineapple juice in a blender or liquidizer. Add 6 ice cubes and whizz until smooth. To serve, drizzle a little raspberry syrup down the sides of 2 tall glasses, pour in the blended fruit and ice mixture and stir well. Serve immediately.

lemon
ice cream soda

The original "float" was invented during the late 19th century in the US. I like this version where the ingredients are blended together before serving. You can top with extra scoops of ice cream, if liked.

⅓ cup lemon squash (undiluted)
1½ oz. freshly squeezed lemon juice
½ oz. sugar syrup
a large scoop of vanilla ice cream
crushed ice
finely pared lemon peel, to garnish

serves 1

❄

Put the lemon squash and juice, sugar syrup, and ice cream in a blender or liquidizer. Add 2 scoops crushed ice and whizz until smooth. Spoon into a chilled martini glass, garnish with a few shreds of lemon peel and serve immediately.

Mix up a creamy Surf Rider and you'll be transported to a Caribbean beach with crystal clear, turquoise waves lapping at the shore. For a tangy treat, try this frozen version of a Mojito (see page 73)—it makes a light granita-style ice that's perfect served as a summer dessert.

surf rider

2 oz. Malibu (coconut-flavored rum)
2 oz. fresh pineapple juice
2 oz. coconut milk
a small handful of fresh mint leaves
1 oz. dark rum
crushed ice

serves 2

Put the Malibu, pineapple juice, coconut milk, and mint in a blender or liquidizer and whizz until smooth. Spoon the mixture into 2 chilled cocktail glasses and float the dark rum over the top by pouring it in over the back of a spoon. Serve immediately.

mojito slush

1 cup superfine sugar
leaves from 1 large bunch of fresh mint, finely chopped, plus extra to garnish
½ cup Bacardi or other white rum
freshly squeezed juice of 4 limes
½ cup sparkling water
an ice cream machine

serves 4

Put the sugar and ⅔ cup water in a saucepan and heat until the sugar has completely dissolved. Let the mixture bubble for 1–2 minutes until slightly syrupy. Remove from the heat, stir in the mint and leave to infuse until cold. Strain the mixture to remove the mint, then stir in the rum, lime juice, and sparkling water. Churn in an ice cream machine until frozen, then transfer to a freezerproof container and freeze. When ready to serve, spoon into tall glasses and garnish with chopped mint.

This treat is inspired by the Indian yogurt drink, lassi. Simply freeze fresh fruit juice in an ice cube tray and serve with a glass of yogurt for a delicious chilled treat.

fruit ice cubes with yogurt

2 cups fresh fruit juice or juice blend of your choice
½ cup plain yogurt
sparkling water, to top up
ice cube trays

makes 18-24
depending on size of ice tray used

Fill the ice cube trays with fruit juice and freeze for at least 1 hour. When ready to serve, fill tall glasses with the frozen juice cubes, add a generous spoonful of the yogurt and top up with sparkling water. Serve immediately.

The vibrant red of the raspberry sauce makes a pretty topping to this creamy vanilla ice. This is guaranteed to be a big hit with the kids.

vanilla ice with raspberry ripple

2 cups full-fat milk
1⅓ cups single cream
1 vanilla bean, split lengthwise
½ cup superfine sugar
1 cup frozen raspberries, thawed
2–3 tablespoons confectioners' sugar

serves 6

Put the milk, cream, vanilla bean, and sugar in a saucepan. Heat to a simmer and then continue cooking for a further 5 minutes, stirring until the sugar has dissolved. Remove from the heat. When the mixture is cool, scrape the black vanilla seeds into the mixture and discard the bean. Transfer the mixture to a freezerproof container and put in the freezer for 4 hours. Break the mixture up with a fork and return it to the freezer for a further 3–4 hours.

Mix the raspberries and confectioners' sugar together and pass through a fine strainer. Take the vanilla ice out of the freezer and let it sit for 10 minutes before scooping into sundae glasses. Drizzle with the raspberry purée to serve.

To save a few minutes, you can simply blend all the ingredients for this shake together in one go, but I like the rippled effect of swirling the peach and raspberry flavors together just before serving. Both taste equally good.

peach melba ripple

4 peach halves, canned in juice, drained
1 teaspoon vanilla extract
2 cups full-fat milk
4 scoops of vanilla ice cream
½ pint fresh raspberries

serves 2

Put the peach halves, half the vanilla extract, half the milk, and 2 scoops of vanilla ice cream in a blender or liquidizer. Whizz until smooth and divide between 2 frosted tumblers. Repeat with the raspberries and remaining vanilla extract, milk, and ice cream. Drizzle the raspberry mixture carefully into the glasses to give a rippled effect. Serve immediately.

Sharp and tangy, this rich confection is just like cheesecake in a glass. If you serve it with a graham cracker or ginger cookie, you almost have the real thing!

lemon cheesecake shake

4 oz. cream cheese
finely grated peel and freshly squeezed juice of ½ lemon
4 tablespoons lemon curd
½ cup Greek-style yogurt
1 cup full-fat milk

serves 4

Put the cream cheese, grated lemon peel and juice, lemon curd, yogurt, and milk in a blender or liquidizer and whizz until smooth. Pour into frosted tumblers and serve immediately.

A recent addition to the fabulous range of gourmet chocolate bars now available is "chile chocolate." It has quite a kick to it and makes the ideal ingredient for an instant spicy chocolate drink that is great hot, but even better frozen and served as a granita.

long island milkshake

This milkshake is for adults only—don't be fooled by the innocent name!

½ oz. vodka
½ oz. gin
½ oz. white rum
½ oz. tequila
½ oz. triple sec
a squeeze of fresh lemon juice
⅓ cup cola
2 large scoops of vanilla ice cream
crushed ice

serves 1

Put all the spirits, lemon juice, cola, and ice cream in a blender or liquidizer with 2 scoops of crushed ice and whizz until smooth. Pour into a tall frosted glass and serve immediately.

chile chocolate granita

2 cups full-fat milk
4 oz. chile-flavored chocolate
broken into pieces
grated bittersweet chocolate, to garnish
candied chile, to garnish (optional)

serves 4

Put the milk in a saucepan and heat gently until simmering. Remove from the heat and stir in the chocolate pieces until melted. Set aside to cool.

Pour the mixture into a shallow metal pan, cover closely with plastic wrap and then freeze for 2–3 hours, until slightly slushy. Break up with a fork and then freeze for a further 4 hours.

Take the granita out of the freezer and let it sit for 10 minutes, before scooping into sundae glasses. Sprinkle with grated chocolate and candied chile, if using, and serve immediately.

When I was a child the weekly visit from the ice cream van was a thrilling experience. My favorite was a Cider Barrel lolly. This Cider Apple Slushie attempts to replicate the flavor but, unlike the lolly, contains real cider so it's an adults-only treat. The Piña Colada is a thick, tropical treat—for a child-friendly version, simply omit the rum.

cider apple slushie

3 large cooking apples, peeled, cored, and sliced
1 quart sweet cider
1 cup sugar
2 cinnamon sticks, lightly bashed
thinly sliced apple, to garnish (optional)

serves 4

Put the apple slices, cider, sugar, and cinnamon sticks in a saucepan and bring slowly to a boil, stirring until the sugar has dissolved. Cover and simmer gently for 12–15 minutes until the apples are soft.

Remove from the heat and leave to cool. When cool, remove the cinnamon sticks and discard. Transfer the mixture to a blender or liquidizer. Whizz until smooth, then spoon into a freezerproof container and freeze for 4–6 hours.

To serve, return the mixture to the blender and whizz briefly. Pour into tall glasses, garnish with apple slices, if using, and serve immediately.

iced piña colada

10 oz. fresh ripe pineapple, chopped
⅓ cup sugar
1 cup coconut milk
4 tablespoons white rum
an ice cream machine

serves 2

Put the pineapple in a bowl, add the sugar and mix well. Leave to stand at room temperature for 10 minutes to allow the sugar to dissolve into the chopped pineapple.

Put all the ingredients in an ice cream machine and churn until just softly slushy. Pour into frosted glasses and serve immediately.

In Italy, coffee granita is served in tall glasses topped with whipped cream for a refreshing summer aperitif, but this version makes a great summer dessert.

coffee granita

1 quart freshly-made espresso coffee
1¼ cups sugar
a little whipped cream and ground cinnamon, to serve

serves 8

Make the coffee using whatever method you prefer and while the coffee is still hot, stir in the sugar until dissolved. Leave to cool and then transfer to a freezerproof container.

Freeze the mixture for 1–2 hours, until ice crystals have formed around the edges of the coffee syrup. Stir well and return to the freezer for a further 2–3 hours, stirring every hour until almost frozen.

Fork over the granules and spoon into iced glasses. Top with whipped cream and dust with cinnamon to serve. You'll need spoons!

chai vanilla milkshake

1 quart full-fat milk
⅓ cup light muscovado sugar
2 tablespoons black tea leaves
1 vanilla bean, split lengthwise
¼ teaspoon ground cinnamon
8 cardamom pods
¼ teaspoon ground allspice
3 scoops of vanilla ice cream
ice cube trays

serves 4

Put 3 cups of the milk, the sugar, tea leaves, vanilla bean, cinnamon, cardamom, and allspice in a saucepan and bring to a boil. Reduce the heat and simmer gently for 5 minutes, then turn off the heat, cover and leave for 10 minutes. Strain into the ice cube trays and freeze until solid. When ready to serve, put the frozen chai cubes in a blender or liquidizer with the remaining milk and the ice cream and whizz until smooth. Serve immediately.

index

recipe credits

Louise Pickford

Alabama slammer
Berry cordial
Blueberry cordial with fizzy
apple juice
Bondi rip
Chile chocolate granita
Chocatini
Cider apple slushie
Classic sangria
Coffee granita
Cosmopolitan iced tea
Cranberry and fruit punch
Cranberry, lemon, and ginger iced tea
Elderflower and berry cup
Fruit martinis
Ginger beer, lime, and mint crush
Gingerella punch
Hamptons hangover
Hollywood hustle
Iced pear sparkle
Jasmine and lychee iced tea
Lemon cheesecake shake
Lemon ice cream soda
Lemon, lime, and bitters
Long Island milkshake
Long Island iced tea
Mandarin caprioska
Mango and berry pash
Mango, raspberry, and
cranberry cruise
Melon, cucumber, and sweet
ginger frappé
Orange sunset
Passion fruit and orange cordial
Passion fruit rum punch

Peach melba ripple
Peach and strawberry sangria
Pomegranate syrup and lemonade
Raspberry, apple, and lychee juice
Raspberry and apple fizz
Sea freeze
Strawberry, rose, and vanilla iced tea
Surf rider
Tennessee teaser
Vanilla ice with raspberry ripple
Watermelon kick
Watermelon and pear frothy

❋

Ben Reed

Brazilian mule
Caipirinha
Chocmint Martini
Classic margarita
Cranberry Cooler
Jamaican breeze
Mai tai
Mangorita
Mint julep
Mojito
Original daiquiri
Planter's punch
Raspberry rickey
Rum runner
Sea breeze
Shirley Temple
St. Clement's
Strawberry mule
T-punch
Virgin Mary
Vodka collins

Elsa Petersen-Schepelern

Apple lemonade
Apricot, berry, and orange juice
Blueberry and orange juice
Fruit ice cubes with yogurt
Gingered pear juice
Iced lime tea
Melon frothy
Moroccan iced mint tea
Pimm's
Pomegranate squeeze
Rhubarb berryade

❋

Sunil Vijayaker

Crushed ice sticks with fruit cordial
Fruity ice sticks
Iced piña colada

❋

Liz Franklin

Ice cream ice cubes for sodas
Mojito slush

❋

Tonia George

Chai vanilla milkshake
Iced peach and elderflower tea

❋

Susannah Blake

Frothy iced coffee

❋

Brian Glover

Homemade fresh lemonade

photography credits

All photographs by *William Lingwood*
unless otherwise stated below:

❋

Richard Jung
Pages 20, 21, 26, 33, 58, 74, and 91

❋

Ian Wallace
Pages 29, 32, 34, 36, 38, and 86

❋

Martin Brigdale
Pages 9 and 92

❋

Francesca Yorke
Page 69

❋

Prop styling *Rachel Jukes* and home economy *Lucy McKelvie*
for all photographs except the following: 9, 20, 21, 23, 26, 29,
30, 31, 32, 33, 34, 36, 38, 40, 43, 57, 58, 62, 68, 69, 71, 72, 73,
74, 75, 76, 79, 83, 84, 86, and 92